ADULT DEPARTMENT

1. Fine Schedule
   1- 5 days overdue . . . . grace period, no fine
   6-10 days overdue . . . . 25¢ per item
   11-19 days overdue . . . . 75¢ per item
   20th day overdue . . . . $2.00 per item
2. Injury to books beyond reasonable wear and all
   losses shall be paid for.
3. Each borrower is held responsible for all books
   drawn on his card and for all fines accruing on
   the same.

FOND DU LAC PUBLIC LIBRARY
FOND DU LAC, WISCONSIN

The
Religious Impulse

The
Religious Impulse

by
Jean-Claude Barreau

translated by
John George Lynch, C.S.P., Ph.D.

Paulist Press
New York/Ramsey

Library of Congress
Catalog Card Number: 78-71436

ISBN: 0-8091-2186-7

Cover design: Salem Tamer

Published by Paulist Press
Editorial Office: 1865 Broadway, New York, N.Y. 10023
Business Office: 545 Island Road, Ramsey, N.J. 07446

Printed and bound in the
United States of America

Contents

Translator's Preface

When David Yount, a friend of mine, first met Jean-Claude Barreau, he said, "Did you notice his eyes? I imagine Camus' eyes must have looked like that." I never mentioned that observation to Jean-Claude Barreau; I suspect he would have preferred comparison to deGaulle or Mauriac or Malraux. Even more so, he would have preferred: "I imagine Jesus' eyes must have looked like that." Some would call them haunted eyes; I choose to say they are restless, much as Augustine's heart was "restless until it rested in God."

If you have read any of Barreau's books previously translated into English, you know something of the fire and passion in his words. Barreau's restlessness is a delight to read, a joy, a delight to share. Like fire, it gives off both heat and light. Like passion, he engages.

His thoughts come quickly. Translating him is like translating a fire—sometimes a roaring blast, like a blaze in a furnace—sometimes quieter and gentler, like a campfire in a hidden wood. Even when he burns, the wounds heal and new wisdom rises from the ashes.

If there ever were such a bird as the phoenix, it would be Barreau's bird. As it is, he prefers the eagle or the hawk—and, paradoxically, the tiny "red throats" that flit about the streams near his ancestral home not far from Vendome, west of Paris. I have ridden with him there as he galloped his stallion Étan through the ancient forests, his wife Ségolene at his side. Astride that marvelous, foamed, and sweaty animal, he once turned to me and said: "You cannot stay in France; you are too much at ease here—a Christian can never be that much at ease."

In the latter chapters of this book, I learned years later what he had meant. I had made France my idol, and francophilia my "contraband" religion. He was not belittling my ingrained patriotism for his native land, but, like Luther, he insisted that God—and only God—be God. Read on, and you will see what I mean. Remember, though, you are reading a fire. Ideas will leap up and then die away almost as quickly as you saw them. Insights will linger on like burning embers. When you finish, you will know you have been touched; you will not know exactly how for some time to come. That's how Barreau is—both as a writer and as a man.

I have decided to dedicate this translation to his son, Matthew, aged five at this writing, a grand de-

votee of his father, his mother, and American cow-
boys, in that order.

John George Lynch, C.S.P., Ph.D.
Washington, D.C.
January, 1978

We Cannot Get Rid of Religion

My grandfather Barreau never really thought of himself as a religious man. He died in 1953 at the age of eighty-eight, but I still remember his free-thinking, mustached figure—the dominant influence in my childhood and adolescence. Not a large man, he held himself proudly, and his sharp eyes often cast a righteously angry gaze across a cloud-less sky. "The clericals built this temple," he would say to me, pointing to the basilica of the Sacred Heart, its dome dominating our neighborhood, "to humiliate the people they conquered." He was an anti-clerical; his own father had defended the Com-mune of Paris in 1870; ostensibly, at least, he never entered a church to pray. He spoke of a clear, transparent world, and on summer nights he told me of the stars and the marvels of science. Auguste Comte's "Law of the Three Estates" was beyond discussion. Religion was a thing of the past, and reason reigned supreme. What remnant of religion remained had rotted, and it smelled bad. He loved to cite Victor Hugo: "Humanity rises and totters to its feet—its forehead bathed in shadows, it marches toward the dawn."

Because of him my own feelings about religion as I grew up were far from enthusiastic, but since then I have lived. During the war in Algeria, I saw death. Living among the poor in Paris, I experienced misery too atrocious to be told that ground to dust my grandfather's brilliant world. In loving and being loved I have discovered that religion cannot be sloughed off—it sticks to our skin.

Even my grandfather was a deeply religious man. He adored abstractions—reason, humanity, and science. Even though disincarnate, his religion of reason and progress still set up duties and demanded the supreme sacrifice. Hardly the least poisonous of religions, it helped imprison all who refused to be catalogued or used—madmen, delinquents, the restless, and those marginal to society. Behind my grandfather's mustache lurked Robespierre and the terror of 1789.

For a long time I believed our own era's claim to be the first truly a-religious age. André Malraux chose the break up of religion as one of his favorite themes and regarded the apparent collapse of Christianity as the pathetic end of the religious adventure. From his perspective, religion's soul wore itself out in its greatest effort. Religion, however, has not died. Nor has man's mystical impulse vanished. But for centuries religions have lost their vitality.

2

One simply follows upon the other, and now there is a general crisis of religion, the same sort of degeneration that gave rise to Comte's Three Estates.

I also followed my masters—Marx, Freud, and Nietzsche—who told me that religion was a poisonous illusion already condemned.

The Marxist Critique

John-Paul Sartre once said: "Marx is the horizon of our culture." Marx, of course, maintained that religion was the opium of the people because it alienated man/woman from himself/herself and from his/her world. Driven to her/his limits, religious man/woman projected a mythical ideal in the heavens, swerved from true action, and glued himself/herself to illusory activity. Moreover, said Marx, religion did not possess its own consistency. It was no more than the image of humankind's theoretical struggles, in reality economic and class conflicts. Change the conditions by a socialist-scientific revolution, said the German philosopher-economist, and religion would vanish like a morning fog.

Marx, however, did point out that religion, like all cultural phenomena, springs from specific mentalities and espouses the spirit of its own time. It may disavow its socio-economic roots, but it is always a child of its era. Comte had said the same thing. This observation, however, has its limits, for a religion can retain its own identity in the midst of

3

cultural trappings. Christianity has worn Judaic, Greek, and Roman cloaks; Islam has known Byzantine and Persian forms.

Marx's theory of projection also has its limits. Borrowed from Feuerbach and Hegel, it failed to take into account the fecundity of living religions, their extraordinary creative power in art and in social justice. As an economic genius, Marx remains essential to any study of politics; as a critic of religion, he is a lightweight. Despite his impassioned denunciations of man's/woman's exploitation of man/woman, he brought in his criticism of religion as something smuggled into his thought. Seeking to throw off a Judaism and Christianity long emptied of substance, he denounced a caricature of religion—a spineless, individualistic piety, little more than exhortations to exploited masses to be submissive. His real genius was not in the religious domain.

Marx is not alone as a smuggler of ideas contraband to his thought. When a person demonstrates genius in one domain, society tends to accept all his/her opinions, even in fields clearly behind his/her competency. An hour or two before a TV screen or a radio is proof enough. All sorts of researchers, doctors, botanists, and even long-distance runners give ethical, religious, and philosophical advice. The net result is pure comedy.

With Marx the situation is more like tragedy for we are still far from recovering from his anti-religious spirit. His ethic, for instance, is really nothing but stoicism which he borrowed from 18th century France.

One can hardly reproach Marx himself—he was not an ethicist. The tragic result of his ethic remains evident, however, in the bourgeois moral attitudes and heavy sexual repression reigning almost everywhere in today's socialist-Marxist regimes. His idea of the state (I am not referring to his unmasking the secret inner workings of the capitalistic state, but to the state he sought to inaugurate through socialism) is really that of a Jacobin of 1789. His criticism of religion springs from the same parentage.

The Freudian Critique

Freud's criticism of religion, sharper and more original, came into my life after Marx's. Plunged into the brutal world of teen-age gangs in Paris, I needed help, and Marc Oraison, Freudian psychologist and friend, came to my aid. Inculcating in me a great respect for the Viennese master, he helped me embrace the Freudian critique of religion.

For Freud, religion was the domain for doing battle with father-figures. In his early days, he offered the theory of projection so common to 19th century thinkers like Feuerbach and Marx. Later, he came to study religion's own enigmatic qualities, especially its affirmation of a father-god and man's relationships of obedience and guilt to that god. To understand religion, Freud latched onto the analysis of paternal relationships. In *The Future of an Illusion*, he explained the forces constantly frustrating man's/woman's desires: the hostile powers of the external world, the irresolvable conflict between

5

the individual and society, and the ever-present threat of death. Narcissism, he said, then took over, and the human person began to believe in the omnipotence of his/her own desires. To avoid these hostile forces, man/woman created the infantile image of an omnipotent, protective father-god.

Although Freud understood many of the complexities of the religious fact, his hatred of religion, like Marx's, remains highly suspect. Failing to take into account religious phenomena that did not fall into the scope of his criticism, he ignored religions like Hinduism where there is no father-figure. Even in Christianity, the central figure is not a father, but a crucified, dishonored, and pleading man. The focus is on weakness, not on power. Both Freud and Marx overstepped their scientific boundaries in entering into the domain of religion, where, as Kant had said, science has nothing to say.

In every expression of spirituality, whether in an individual or a work of art, Freud cried out: "Repressed sexuality!" If the expression could not be interpreted immediately as evidently sexual, it then became "psychosexual." Carl Jung remembered well Freud's saying: "My dear Jung, promise me you will never abandon the sexual theory. It is fundamental. You see, it must become a dogma, an impregnable bastion." (The tone of his remarks sounds like a mother telling her son: "Promise me you will go to Mass every Sunday of your life!") When Jung asked: "A bastion against what?" Freud replied, "Against the black waves, against the occult." By the occult, Jung noted, Freud seemed to mean all religion and all philosophy. Freud, who warred incessantly against religion, seems never to have been asked why his hatred of religion was so intense. Analyst, analyze thyself!

The Nietzschean Critique

Lest my thought begin to sound too strange, I must now present the third master I knew as a young pagan—Nietzsche. In a certain sense, his criticism of religion pleased me the most. I was convinced that Christianity had de-virilized mankind. In fact, the degenerate Christianity that Nietzsche stigmatized, even though it was not Christianity in its truest form, had done just that. Emmanuel Mounier once referred to his fellow Christians as "slouching beings who move through life from bias to bias . . . Sunday dreamers . . . devotional cowards." I used to tremble with horror at the great blaspheming cry: "God is dead," without realizing that the death of God is in no way the death of religion.

I now believe that Nietzsche's relationship with religion has been enormously misunderstood. Certainly his ultra-rationalistic criticism of religion, belonging part and parcel to the 19th century, has no pretense of being scientific. But his words bear meaning just the same. His disturbing religious spirit, a seductive mixture of mystical atheism and the worst of the religions of power and instinct, enabled Nazism to win countless followers, whatever Nietzscheans may say to the contrary. Young

7

people, naturally Nietzschean because naturally fascist, retain his sense of sacrifice and hard work, his taste for adventure, risk, and power, his devotion to virility, and his defiance of death. Fascism respects all these values so cherished by adolescents, forgetting they need to be integrated into a broader plan. Next to Marxism and its appeal to adult values (understandably so, since communism has never practiced the demagoguery of the young), fascism remains adolescent, cruel, and pitiless. Nietzsche himself remained an adolescent to the end. No one has better expressed the romantic, festive, violent, yet falsely hopeful religion of the young than he. What he criticized was not really religion, but bigotry; he did so flooded with dionysian dreams. He didn't try to destroy divinity—just the Christian God, precisely because he saw Christianity as a religion of slaves. Nietzschean attitudes and behavior among the young never surprises me; prolonged beyond adolescence, they bore me to death.

As I said above, my experiences of death, misery, and love all contributed to the crumbling away of my grandfather's "rational" and "reasonable" world. My eyes opened to the limits of my masters' critiques. True, they did lay bare the illusions passing for true religion. Their own illusion, however, was to think that religion itself was liquidated once its illusion was unveiled.

Gradually I became convinced that one could never do away with religion, a conviction so crucial that all the so-called definitive criticisms of religion began to pale to relativity next to it. I came to see that Marx, Freud, and Nietzsche not only misunderstood religion, but contributed to its repression.

Religion and the Modern World

A quick look at the modern world these thinkers helped shape shows how powerfully Western culture works to repress the religious instinct. The atheism so common to modern Western thinkers (or, more accurately, their total, existential hatred of religion) is not accidental to our culture; atheism is at its very source. As early as 1844, Kierkegaard sensed that the most basic element repressed in our culture was not the instinct for sex, but the instinct for religion.

To Freud we owe much enlightenment about repression. We know that just when we think we have done away with an impulse, it rises up again in some aberrant way and establishes itself very dangerously in its substitute soil. By what blindness did Freud fail to apply this to the religious instinct? Short-sighted explanations, ignoring this fact of repression, write off the apparent decline of religion by reference to weakened faith, ethical easiness, and the scientific spirit. In fact, the 20th century is one of the most religious ages man has known. Because its religions spring from a repression of the religious spirit, they are clandestine and unrecognized. The age, profoundly religious, passes for secular.

Because of the negative consequences of repression so well described by Freud, the two great religions of this century—Nazism and Stalinism—have exercised their reign over thousands of cadavers. The "great red" Nazism that Brassilach adored, with its cathedrals and its lights, captivated the fervor of the German masses to their own destruction. A religion of instinct, blood, and death, it resurrected the ancient Aztec and Assyrian cults. Like them, it had no art, cosmology, or poetry; its dimension of human sacrifice made Assurbanipal look like a kindergarten child in comparison. It was a religion without intellectual content. Suffice to open the pages of its sacred book, *Mein Kampf*, and wonder how this raging nonsense moved so many people? How did such a grotesque high priest, so satanic and delirious as Hitler, come to be adored? How did this occur in the land of Marx, Freud, and Nietzsche? In fact, they were all secret accomplices to this mad genius' thought. With Nazism, the enormous religious power of the Germanic people, still active and alive in Hegel, but repressed by his successors, burst out anew in the crematoriums.

Stalin twisted to his own advantage the messianism of the Russians, the most religious people on the face of the earth. Exalting a mythical proletariat, he then brought in the Gulag. No one, not even party members could escape from this Stalinist hell. Marxism, fundamentally a religion of reason and science, suddenly found itself a shock force in history. Stunned, it contemplated this man-eating religion it had engendered. It would be naive to pin all the blame on Stalin, but next to him the absolutism of the czars seems practically liberal. Compare, for instance, the witnesses of Kropotkin and Dostoevski with those coming from the Gulags.

Those who know Stalinism, with its pilgrimage of Western thinkers to the Kremlin, recognized in Maoism the same ingredients: exaltation of the mythical leader and the people straining toward the radiant future, the golden age. Underneath the myth, of course, lie the heretics, dying in their prison-camp hells. Pasqualini's *Prisoner of Mao* leads one to believe that the Maoist camps were worse than those of Stalin. The Gulags, at least, just ground their men up from the outside—they were free to think as they pleased, so long as nothing resulted from it. The Maoists decreed that each citizen not only speak the truth, but think it as well!

Six million Jews, either deported or burned in the Nazi crematoriums, 20 million Russians massacred in the Gulags (the Soviets themselves admit these figures), and God knows how many Chinese have paid with their lives for the greatest religion explosion in history—or should we not rather call it the great and bloodied explosion of repressed religion? Yes, the traces of this religious repression are footprints bathed in blood.

Perhaps now the meaning behind the title of this book is more clear. If the repression of religion produces such cataclysmic effects, we must learn to live with it. If we can never do away with religion, it is crucial and urgent to use it as best we can.

11

Faith and Religion

Religion had become so discredited in Western culture that even believers wanted no further part of it. If they wanted to believe, how could they? Religion didn't go any place; to be religious was to live on a merry-go-round. Fortunately, Dietrich Bonhoeffer found in Karl Barth the distinction between faith and religion that enabled many believers to find their identity once again. Bonhoeffer, one of the most appealing and significant figures in contemporary Christianity, took his stand against Nazism and died, strangled by the Gestapo. His recognition that Nazism was a religion led him to hold all religion in horror. In keeping with Marx, Freud, and Nietzsche, he maintained that religion was an ambiguous and negative impulse in people, but he said that Christianity was not a religion. It was a faith, a free, personal act to which the criticisms of religion did not apply. Faith, as a free act of confidence in someone else, was the meeting of the God who revealed himself as a person. This God could not be found in the mottled images of religion.

He could be encountered only in faith, the highest, most dynamic, most outreaching act of human consciousness. Faith was the recognition of that surpassing and delicious Other who is God.

Separation of Faith and Religion

The distinction between faith and religion has enjoyed immense popularity in France and in the Anglo-Saxon "Death of God" theologians. Even non-believers have found it useful, claiming that Christianity is finally losing its illusions about itself because it is not really a religion at all, but a faith. Let us speak of faith, they say—raw, de-mystified, and lively.

Defense of religion is no longer acceptable. Jean Danielou wrote that enlightened Christians, capable of faith, had no need for religion. Only the non-enlightened needed religion; otherwise, they would no longer pray. The famous Jesuit cardinal, far from opposing the faith-religion distinction, actually bolstered it with a profoundly conservative class distinction, not much different from Napoleon's belief that, "The people need a religion." I do not believe, however, that religion is for the people and faith for the enlightened. Religion is for everyone, be he/she enlightened or not.

Everything that Bonhoeffer and his disciples have said about religion is excellent, as are their warnings about its dangers. But why reject religion totally and separate it absolutely from faith? This seductively appealing distinction enabled me to

13

bypass the disgust of religion my grandfather had inspired in me to become a Christian without too much trouble, but it is a dangerous dichotomy. Without religion, faith becomes a cerebral act with no effective power, offering people little emotional satisfaction. On the other hand, faith crowns religion as its fullest accomplishment. Without faith, religion falls easy prey to repression and brutal, aberrant behavior. Faith is the best use of religion.

Superstition or Stoicism

For almost a century now, two degenerate forms of religion invading Christian churches make it easy to see why the faith-religion distinction was so attractive. The first, the inclination toward superstition and bigotry, is really less dangerous than the second, the tendency to stoicism in moral theology. With the possible exception of the Orthodox churches, Christian churches have reduced Christianity to a flat and boring ethical system. Marcus Aurelius has replaced Jesus Christ, and the cult of duty and good resolutions the Beatitudes. Children go to catechism classes to learn how to behave, not how to live; liturgies grow more and more cerebral, sermons dry and monotonous.

The boredom young people experience with the Christian churches explains why so many searching for religion look to India, often to what is most alienating in Hinduism. Even the most dishonest gurus find their followers, and the weirdest sects claim their adherents.

Divorced from the main currents of contemporary life, the churches have failed to purify man's/woman's religious torrent. This stream then pours over into swampy land to disappear or explodes in dangerous forms. I have already accused the "Fathers" of contemporary society as responsible for the repression of religion. But precisely where religion finds itself rootless and disinherited, the spiritual bankruptcy of the churches is to blame. Let it not be forgotten: the most intense commitment to religion does not pull a person away from activity, struggle, and daily life. It sends him/her into the foray, stronger and better armed. The collapse of the Christian churches would not be so tragic were they not the sole possessors of a way to use the religious impulse. This way, given to them by Jesus Christ, will be treated in more detail in chapter 7. Now we must ask ourselves: What is the nature of religion?

What is Religion?

Religion as Characteristically Human

When I speak of the religious fact, I mean primarily man's/woman's instinct, impulse, and disposition for adoration. Included in this meaning are both individual mystical desires and the historical organizations that have served to express this fact.

Of all human impulses, religion is the most characteristically human. Although intelligence can be found in the higher strata of mammals, religion is never emblematic of those orders. Even an agnostic like Vercors had to admit this fact. In one of his most beautiful books, he depicts the discovery of a species in-between man and the monkey in a forgotten jungle corner. A scientist kills one of the offspring of this strange species, and a crisis of conscience ensues. Is it truly a child? If so, the killer can be executed. If not, he need only pay a fine to the SPCA. The bewigged judges (the story takes place in England) find to their horror they do not know what is required to be human. Finally, it is

16

proved these creatures are human because they practice religious rites! There was, in the story, no other way to differentiate between humans and animals.

Edgar Morin, in his recent writings, says the same thing: man/woman is not simply "faber" (producer) or "sapiens" (rational); he/she is also "demens" (mad), with a madness for God. Bergson put it this way: " 'Homo sapiens' is the only being endowed with reason; he is also the only being capable of hitching his existence on things beyond reason."

Religion and Sexuality

Although it is the most characteristically human impulse, religion is joined in humankind's heart with two other forces—the sexual and artistic impulses. All are close cousins, but each is different. Sexuality is especially close to religion because it implies personal relationships and an experience of love not unlike faith. Even sexual orgasm enjoys a certain kinship to mystical religious experience. As Pauline Reage writes in her classic study of sado-masochistic eroticism: *The Story of O*: "It's a curious thing, but the simple fact of being flesh-to-flesh with someone, even someone unknown, establishes a kind of communication that is magical and incomprehensible. I have to say it is almost sacred!"

Certainly the pagan religions were filled with sexuality: phallic and vaginal symbols, sacred pros-

17

titution, and the phallus of Delos. The mystics, moreover, use profoundly sexual themes. Often in the Bible God's passionate love is portrayed as battered, deceived, and betrayed by unfaithful but loving humankind. Nor can we forget the marvelous eroticism of the Canticle of Canticles, the most beautiful love poem ever written.

Unlike religion, however, sexuality has a close link with death. A-sexual beings reproduce by dividing themselves and do not experience death; only sexual beings die. Often they experience death as a slow-fused bomb in their hearts, and those who make sexuality their religion find themselves swept into suicide when their sexual powers diminish.

Although religion seeks for an object to be adored, the object of the sexual impulse must remain relative; if I love someone as a god, I do not love him for himself. I love a fantasy, and this kind of love ultimately kills the beloved. Do not the authors of crimes of passion often say: "I killed her because I loved her too much"?

The great historical religions made enormous progress when they began to distinguish religion and sexuality. Separation, however, does not mean repression. Primitive Christianity freed itself from pagan pan-sexualism and maintained a rather healthy attitude toward sexuality. Jesus, for instance, was surrounded by women, not always of irreproachable morals, and he was fond of saying that the prostitutes would precede the Pharisees into the kingdom of heaven. He knew that the worst kind of prostitution was not of the body. Following

18

his example, medieval Christianity was neither prudish nor puritanical. Rabelais, himself, was a priest.

Although Gospel Christianity was not puritanical, Mediterranean misogyny arose as early as St. Paul, and by the Middle Ages the "sins of the flesh" were the most serious of all, despite Jesus' constant proclamation that sin was first of all hypocrisy, bad faith, hatred, and exploitation of one's neighbor. This rigid current would be topped off by mandatory clerical celibacy and the advent of Puritanism, both manifestations of repressed sexuality inverted toward castration and guilt. Pagan pan-sexualism also reappeared in the cults of Mary where the Mother of Jesus was adorned as a Greek goddess. The cult of a Mother-goddess, for instance, existed at Ephesus long before the Church council of the same name.

Coexisting with sexuality, religion need neither repress nor castrate. So long as religion is neither prudish nor puritanical, it helps sexuality's full development and prevents the sexual impulse from closing in on itself.

Both religion and sexuality need aggression to grow. Freud's studies, furthered by Konrad Lorenz, have revealed the importance of this quality in humans and animals alike. Because religion—as an instinct for adoration—implies relationships, it cannot ignore aggression without incurring danger to itself. Nor can sexuality. Both must integrate aggression, since violence is the raw material of gentleness. "The kingdom of God is difficult to enter," said Jesus, "and the violent tear it away." He who called himself the meekest of men did not hesitate to overthrow the money changers' tables and chase the merchants with a whip when the occasion demanded. Jean Paulhan's words are to the point: "Everything happens as if there existed a certain mysterious balance of violence in the world. But we have lost both the taste and the feeling for it."

Overly sentimental education, failing to take aggression in human relationships into account, in no way prepares young people to discipline violence and leaves them defenseless. Even more unbearable is vapid love. Jesus speaks more of forgiveness than of love, for he knew that without forgiveness human relationships of friendship and love were impossible. Love means tearing yourself open and stripping away all the masks. Only through indefinitely renewed forgiveness can such a relationship endure. Unless religion uses aggression to forgive and thereby take by storm the mysterious kingdom Jesus announces, aggression will use religion for holy wars, human sacrifice, and other forms of fanaticism. Aggression, therefore, is at the heart of the religious impulse.

Religion and Art

The religious and artistic impulses have been intermingled from the beginning of human activity. The murals painted in the grottos of Lascaux and Altamira are sacred paintings, and the shamans and sorcerers were the first artists. None of the great religions is without art. A Romanesque church expresses the truth of Christianity better than a multitude of pious discourses, and the mosque of Omeyyades tells more about Islam than any learned treatise. Can there be true religion without art? A partial answer comes from a look at the modern atheistic religions. Neither Nazism nor Stalinism (and more recently Maoism) had any art worthy of the name — no more than the degenerate Christianity of the 19th century with its insipid, sterile, "St. Sulpice" art. The stucco Kolkhoziens of the Soviet crossroads, their eyes fixed glassily on the future, are perfect bed partners for the plastic Sacred Hearts adorning so many sacristies!

Both religion and art are poetic acts. Literature, music, sculpture, architecture, chant, and liturgy are all complex creative activities manifesting how closely art and religion intertwine. The artist, like the religious believer, is something of a mystic. Both see things differently. The aphorism is almost banal: "The artist paints, he enables us to see, and we become aware of how blind we were." The same can be said for the religious believer.

Despite these similarities, religion and art must not be identified. Religion must remain separate from art, lest it become no more than an aesthetical attitude. Art, in its turn, cannot become religion, or the artist will find himself/herself lost in his/her own poetic act, as Nietzsche and Holderlin went mad contemplating the sun long after they had forgotten what it was.

Religion and Language

All three impulses, sexual, artistic, and religious, maintain crucially close ties with language. Sexuality, without language, becomes a purely animal instinct. Art, for its part, is really a language in itself. Religion, because so closely related to human anguish, must make use of language in symbolic and mythical forms. Since language arose in the atmosphere of men/women trying to express the anguish they felt as uprooted beings, it summoned forth their religious impulses, giving them a vision of the world no other impulse could give. It is probably true that language began among higher primates when they were forced from their forests to hostile steppes and began to transmit vital observations to one another (to assure the common hunt, for instance), using signals never dreamed of in their instinctive communications. With language, people no longer live as animals in an environment, but as human beings in a world they can interpret and keep at a distance. No longer mute, they can express their agonies about that world in verbal forms.

Religion and Death

These forms grew especially as symbol and myth, the two major language expressions religion uses to enable men/women to face death. Primary symbols, like air, earth, fire, and water, all help to bring out foundational meanings of the world and its relationships. Myth, unlike symbol, does not exist to bring out meaning so much as to humanize the world, making the environment practical and supportable for human relationships. Without religion's symbols and myths, humanity's relationships remain strangely rootless. Centuries of monotheism have planted in us the idea that the fundamental relationship is with God, but nothing could be farther from the truth. Religion implies, first of all, relationship with a concrete, tangible world. Without religion, man/woman can neither be situated in that world nor surmount his/her anxiety about it. Even though religious myth and symbol spring from humankind's death-anxiety, they are fundamentally life-promoting, for they give man/woman the capacity to become aware of death and thereby make him/her the only creature whose place in the universe is neither fixed nor determined.

Religious myth and symbol do not speak simply to that biological death we call the "end of our lives." Death is also a certain way of not living—or of living as if dead. The essential religious question today is not: "Is there life after death?" but "Is there life after birth?" Only in religious language can man/woman find a satisfactory answer. Responses found in the realm of intellectual understanding alone give rise to little more than religious spiritualism. The true religious response is in the realm of the practical, for true religion creates men and women who live in the real world! And the victory over death is true religion's sublimest hope. Is this hope soundly grounded? Only religion can give that answer, and from this challenge religion throws out comes Pascal's famous wager: "God or nothing."

Jesus, of course, proposed that a "tree is known by its fruits" so that if a religion allows people to live while taking death into full account, it is undeniably positive. Modern culture, burying its head in the sand and trembling in fear of death, represses not only biological death, but that death of the soul the religions never deny. Strange how in this century of Nazi concentration camps and Soviet Gulags we pretend there is neither hell nor sin. The smoke of Hiroshima has hardly cleared away, but we conjure away that slaughter like a child's dream. Dying patients, too, seeking to meet death face to face, receive only murky words in return for their requests. A century ago, when a peasant was about to die, he called in his family and friends to settle his affairs and die in peace. I remember my grandfather, brought to peace by his religion of progress, whispering to me the night before he died: "There is no more oil in the lamp." Today he would have died stuffed full of tranquilizers, alone in an anonymous hospital room.

Only the religious man/woman can look death squarely in the face. In his/her deepest heart, he/she senses a life-giving desire that death can be conquered, and this desire is the most profound source for the religious impulse. It is not Freud's libido, the sexual impulse for union using both guilt and anxiety in its victory over death. Romain Rolland speaks of it as "an oceanic feeling . . . a feeling

24

for the eternal." Jung also attributed positive value to the religious desire. Norman O. Brown, in his turn, rejected Freud's idea that the fundamental experience of happiness was to be found in a union prompted by the fear of death. In *Eros and Thanatos* Brown set out to prove that only in religious and mystical experience could man/woman fully realize his/her psychic constitution. For my part, the desire to adore seems far more fundamental to the formation of religion than Oedipal sexual repression.

Buddha, as we shall see, failed in his attempt to preach the extermination of desire. Judaeo-Christianity, on the other hand, is primarily a religion of desire. Its language is filled with longing: "As the heart longs for the streams of living water . . . as the land thirsts for rain . . . as the watchman awaits the dawn." In Christianity, man/woman longs for his/her Absolute; hoping against hope, he/she overcomes all his/her deaths.

The question now arises: Does this desire look to a real object, or is it simply a tendency toward the illusory? Only faith, lived out in religion as commitment, experience, and wager, can respond.

The Best and the Worst

For thousands of years the religious impulse has been organized into cultural systems called religions. Unfortunately, these systems have often expressed what has been suppressed in humanity's religious desires. Bergson saw in religion the "cooling of what mysticism had deposited in the human soul." Some of these religions have been atheistic; others, more political messianisms or social millenarianisms, are even anti-religious.

Many theories exist to explain similarities in these religions. "Evolutionary" theories seek to explain religious facts common to different cultures by suggesting a common origin and common development for all religions. "Diffusionism" claims the elements are carried over from one culture to another. "Psychologism" interprets the convergence of religious facts by reference to psychological mechanisms permanent in the human person. "Phenomenology" maintains that the analogous characteristics in religions prove that within man/

woman lies a unique religious phenomenon transcending all its particular expressions. "Functionalism," highly critical of religion, finds the meaning of religious facts simply in the function they have within their own cultural world. For someone like Claude Lévi-Strauss, for example, only the structures of society have meaning. Religious facts, meaningless apart from structure, have only accidental, analogous significance and depend upon the similarity of underlying structure for their meaning. Each of these interpretative systems has its merits and drawbacks. All of them must be used to throw light on the religions, themselves so complex that any attempt to understand them unilaterally would be risky and foolish.

The history of religions usually begins with a consideration of the great pagan religions with their adoration of the universe. Under the masks of Zeus, Dionysius, Sivakali, and the multitude of animistic deities and genies hides an extremely muddled perception of the universe. In their murky understanding of the depth and poetry of things, these religions see everything as nature's dance. Within every experience, however humble or routine, lies a religious experience and the possibility for wonder. Despite this optimistic elan, the pagan religions never found anything to adore that was able to overcome death. They simply backed away from the fact that everything passes, dies, and disappears. So it was that two other rather desperate attempts at religion appeared about the same time as the pagan religions.

The Buddhist Experience of Society

The first arose in India with Buddha, the first atheist. Raised by his father in a very reassuring religion where suffering and death had no play, one day the young prince peered through the windows of his father's dream palace and discovered another side of life: he saw the poor, the sick, and a cadaver on its way to a funeral pyre. Like all adolescents, including Jesus, he tripped a bit on his own path. Telling himself that his father had deceived him, he left the palace and the young girl he was supposed to marry. Up to this point Buddha's story is common enough. He is one of a host of sheltered young people who finally say: "The world of my parents is a deception." But Buddha went one step further to the most extreme consequences of negation. His long meditation led him to reject Indian paganism, and he came to believe that everything depended upon the reality of death. The human person could find dignity only in refusing all the appearances of life and accepting nothingness as the absolute. Even though life's joys and sufferings were but illusions, there was nothingness to be adored. Little by little it would be filled with some kind of reality. The Buddhist experience is profoundly modern; Men and women of our time are also tempted to leave a deceiving society for some sort of Nirvana. Society, they feel, is decomposing and its abundance is not protecting them from death. Typical is Lévi-Strauss' remark that since Buddha nothing essential has been said.

Plato and Idealism

The second appeared in Greece, where an apparently more positive system replaced paganism. Plato taught that beyond the inconstant, sensible world dwelt pure, immutable, eternal ideas perceptible only as vague reflections in our cavern here below. Platonic idealism was to enjoy considerable success. Although moderately tempered by Aristotle's dualism, it remains the religion of many of our contemporaries. Many Christians, in fact, are idealists without knowing it. Even my grandfather, when he dreamed of reason and science as his religion, was fundamentally a Platonic idealist.

Together with Jesus, Buddha and Plato remain the giants in the history of humankind's religions. All the great religions can be categorized as Buddhist, Platonic, or Christian. Other religious leaders were certainly prophets and wise men, but none found such powerful responses to the problem of evil and the fact of death as these three masters.

Other Religious Wise Men

Zoroaster and Mani, in pitting a god of evil against a god of good, were led inevitably to place the world of imperfection and suffering within the province of the god of evil with the result that life itself came to be detested and abhored. What a sinister world such a religious system would have built. The Albigensians in 12th century France were disciples of this thought.

Abraham and Mohammed both gave witness to an all-powerful god who demanded submission. "Islam," in fact, means "submission." But if God is all-powerful he is then ultimately responsible for everything, including the deaths of the innocent. With Dostoevski and Camus, let us affirm once and for all that it is impossible to adore a god who wills an infant's death.

Socrates and Confucius were both wise men who, like the Stoics after them, taught the dignity of man/woman, but their ethical systems fell far short when face to face with death. More enticing are the great spiritual writers and thinkers filled with their "rush" experiences—the Indian Bagava-Djita and the Chinese Tao. Theirs is the witness to the devouring fires, violent winds, and turbulent seas behind all reality. Allowing themselves to be filled with these forces, they brim over in their lyrical texts; but they are poets, not guides.

The Originality of Jesus

Only Buddha, Plato, and Jesus help man/woman look death in the face, defy it, and conquer it. Buddha offers disdain as his reaction to death; Plato, intelligence and understanding; Jesus, love. The most original of the three, Jesus alone speaks of a God whom we can love not because he is all-powerful, but because he is all-weak. If God is love, says Jesus, he is so in freedom and weakness, as a lover with his beloved. In no way is he responsible for evil; on the contrary, he is on the side of the victim, the tortured, and the ridiculed. From this position he begs our love. "I am before the door, and I knock," proclaim the Gospels, speaking of God, "if someone hears my voice and opens the door, I will enter his house and dine with him." The seeking God of Jesus Christ is the only God to whom modern man/woman could open his/her door. Alas, for centuries now, the Christian churches have done everything but preach the Gospel of this God. They educate and moralize, but they proclaim Jesus Christ and the God of love so little that they remain the great unknowns of our day.

Not only the Christian churches, of course, experience this falling away of their original spirit. All religions, as soon as they institutionalize, tend to smother the very instinct that gave them birth. The religious instinct, after all, is dangerous, explosive, and irruptive; we can never be exactly sure where it will go. The great religions, trying to discipline that impulse and draw out of it what is best, tend to become heavy, and over-bearing in their moralizing, rational, and clerical ways. Forgetting their own charism of service, they make the religious impulse serve them. The impulse then abandons the institution and arises elsewhere, often in dangerous and aberrant forms.

Religion Enriches Life

Religion, however, is not simply impulse, instinct, or desire. A religion's theology is of fundamental importance, for its ideology can be liberating or imprisoning for the religious force. A false sense of ecumenism, interested in putting all doctrine on the same footing, is really little more than degenerate syncretism and leads to loss of the critical spirit, negation of the person, and disinterest in the struggles of daily life. Because the religious impulse is so clouded today in syncretistic forms, the great risk in our society is not revolution, but personal disintegration and suicide. The person who believes in nothing ends up by doing nothing. Young people, for instance, find living tasteless and seek its substitute in drugs and other marginal life experiences. Only authentic religion can bring back a taste for life.

Some years ago I met André Malraux. I can still hear his hoarse voice and see his twitching face: "What bothers an agnostic like me most, my friend," he said, "is that it seems—yes, it seems, that man cannot live without the transcendent . . . something transcendent." This is my conviction, too, and it is the reason for this book. But two fundamental questions still remain: 1) How can the religious instinct be kept on a good path away from the "contraband" religions? 2) Are there criteria for choosing among all the religions the one most truly liberating and enriching?

The Contraband Religions

Harvey Cox, in his now famous *Secular City*, sang the praises of the modern city freed from the noxious influence of religion, wed only to rational understanding and secular action, yet wide open for faith. Like so many contemporary theologians, Cox upheld the distinction between faith and religion. Unfortunately, even the most advanced theologians, like the churches themselves, are generally about one war behind the times. The "secular city" was the dream of the 19th century, the great hope of men like my grandfather. It never did exist. If it exists today in the society dominated by computers and the thirst for information, it is not a city without religion. Paradoxically, the emphasis on computerized knowledge, by taking the attention of people away from rationality and logic —in fact, by delivering them from attention at all—has let loose enormous religious forces. The secular city is filled with idols: the state, the party, law and order, profit, revolution, science and reason, and ethics. Because these idols smuggle the religious spirit into false systems, I call them the "contraband" religions.

This smuggling of the religious impulse has an old name—idolatry—and the Jewish prophets understood it well. Long before Jesus, they saw that if adoration stopped at any earthly reality, it imprisoned man/woman. Living in a world saturated with pagan religiosity, they constantly reminded their people they would perish in slavery if they filled their world with gods and overlords. Theirs was an infinitely easier task than prophets have today, for their idolatries were recognizably religious. Today's, cloaked in secular dress, are not.

In bygone days, for instance, the state was not a clandestine idol. It was to be adored, and it monopolized religious cult. From the Pharaohs to the Persian sovereigns, kings wished to be venerated as gods. Classical Greece, because it laicized the state, was considered democratic, although it had little about it we would call democratic today—neither women nor slaves had rights, but at least the state was no longer adored. The citizens (a minority of the total population) considered themselves free men who owed cultic rights only to the gods. With Alexander and the Greek-Persian synthesis that then became hellenistic culture, the state became divine once again, and the proud Macedonians were obliged to bow in adoration before their king. Imperial Rome, also a state religion, persecuted the early Christians precisely because they refused to render cult to Caesar. Today, we say we have laicized the state, but state religion and worship of the leader were characteristic marks of Nazi paganism and the "socialisms" promoted by Stalin and Mao. They all had their priests, their cult of personality, their rites, and even human sacrifice.

When the religious impulse becomes identified with patriotism, it idolizes the state, and the homeland becomes the absolute to which everything is sacrificed—"my country, right or wrong, but my country!" Millions of cadavers now mixed with the earth in battlefields around the globe testify to the danger that exists when religion becomes patriotism and nothing more. However great its risks and perils, the state remains necessary to human societies unless man/woman wishes to live in a jungle. But the state's apparatus must be as light as possible lest it be adored as divine.

Communism: A Contraband Religion

The Communist party, despite its avowed atheism, is also one of today's contraband religions. A former head of the Communist spy network in occupied Europe, summed it up well: "The party can never err; it can never be wrong. It is always right—it is sacred. Whatever the party says through its secretary is Gospel. To disapprove what the party says is sacrilege. Outside the party there is no salvation. If you are not for it, you are against it." Robrieux, in his biography of Maurice Thorez, former head of the French Communist party, shows how Thorez calumniated and excluded his best friends on pretexts he knew to be false. But he acted under obedience. Refusing to see any reality that would tarnish the idolatrous myth, he fell prey to the ultimate foolishness in any religious illusion. Writing to an Italian friend when Khrushchev published his famous list of Stalin's crimes, Thorez said: "What a blow he has given us. Our past is pure and shiny. Why stir up all this mud?" If the religion of the party has not turned its adherents into accomplices or slaves, it takes away any capacity for resistance. "Why did we not cry out when they arrested us?" asked Solzhenitsyn. Eugenia Guinzburg and her husband recall how they both refused to admit their party had disintegrated in the devastating and irrational waves of Stalinism.

The Catholic Church as Institution

The Communist party has often been compared to the Catholic Church. A comparison worn thin by overuse, it remains accurate to show how the religious impulse can be misused by one or another institution. In its beginnings, the Church, like the party, sought to be an organization of service, but it soon sought its own goals, made itself sacred, and built up an enormous clerical apparatus. Its service had been to the truth, but it soon began to choose between what was good to say and what was not. Like all clericalized structures, it became wary of raw information and chose only truth that would be good for people to hear. After all, "it is not good to speak *all* the truth." Earlier this century, Léon Bloy settled his account with this aphorism: "Not all truth is good to speak. There are even more which are better not heard. A truth that would expose its witness to some disgrace evidently would not be good to speak, and unpleasant truth is better off left alone. All this is fine, but then comes this strange event: if we suppress both dangerous and unpleasant truth, I don't see where there remains a third category. Let us then declare without compromise: It is not good to speak any truth at all! This is what the saying really means. Perhaps there is no truth. Pilate saw it face to face, and he wasn't too sure." In the clerical view of things, only those in positions of responsibility have the right to know reality; ordinary folk are supposed to be too weak to support the facts—precisely the Stalinistic attitude. In the Stalinistic party and in the Catholic Church, access to knowledge is proportionate to grade level: only the highest echelons have the right to exact information. To the extent that an institution's message is essential to humankind it runs its risk of clericalization and sacralization. A fishermen's guild runs little risk of deifying itself. But the party, interested in people's temporal happiness, and the Church, looking to man or woman's spiritual well-being, quickly tend to create their own happiness first of all. The more burning the hopes, the greater this risk. Both the party and the Church fabricate a universe of immobility and conformity to persecute the prophets in their midst. With growth comes the inclination toward conservatism and reaction under the guise of law and order.

Law and Order as Contraband Religion

Law and order can itself become a contraband religion once it becomes sacred in itself. Dictators, tyrants, and totalitarian masters of all times have succeeded not so much by police or military terror as by capitalizing on the need people have to be consoled and reassured. Authentic religion, following Marcuse's beautiful phrase, "pacifier of existence," knows there can be no true consolation without first listening to and freeing the human spirit. Contraband religion seeks to console by demanding submission to external authority. The route is less arduous that way—how light, after all, **the yoke of slavery! Dostoevski's Grand Inquisitor** understood well anguished humanity's propensity to turn everything over to the master's hands. "Men are children," the Inquisitor says to Christ, "they want to be re-assured, and you upset them with your calls to liberty and conscience." Party and Church alike misuse religion when they become servants of the law. Listen to Georges Bernanos, despite his extreme rightist views, stigmatize the powerful Spanish bishops, devoted servants to the religion of law and order during that country's tragic civil war: "The night before, two hundred inhabitants of the small village of Manocor, judged suspect by the Italians, were pulled from their beds in the middle of the night, led by groups to the cemetery, shot in the head, and then burned in a heap. The person whom the niceties of good order obliges me to call the archbishop had delegated one of his priests to distribute absolutions between the volleys. He did so, his shoes wet with blood. I do not want to dwell on the details of this religio-military manifestation. I want simply to point out that this massacre of the poor and defenseless did not provoke one word of blame or protest, not even the most inoffensive word of reservation, from the ecclesiastical authorities. They were content to organize thanksgiving processions." Although Marxism has vigorously denounced this religion of law and order, with the gospel of submission to established power, it has wasted no time in establishing the same religion once it has come into power.

Since the beginnings of capitalism (and perhaps even long before), the profit motive has helped fan the flames of law and order. Often hidden under the veil of noble ideas, the golden calf is the true god of the ruling classes. Even among many distinguished economists, profit receives adoration. The more profit is cut off from any notion of social usefulness, the more it becomes idolatrous, leading to the American way of judging everything—art, men, and women—according to financial worth. The cult of business (an euphemism for the cult of money and profit) has always been a contraband religion. Leon Bloy put it this way: "Of all the commonplace sayings, ordinarily so respectable and so severe, I think 'business is business' is the gravest and most august. It is the central point, the century's culminating word. It must be understood, but this understanding is not given to all men. Poets and artists understand it badly. Those whom we archaically call heroes and saints do not understand it at all. The 'business' of salvation or honor, spiritual 'business,' or the 'business' of the state are not really 'business.' They could all be described in some other way. To be 'in business,' after all, is to be in an absolute!"

The Religion of Profit

Never has the religion of profit been so brutally dominant as today. In medieval Christianity the possession of money carried with it certain duties—the rich man had to protect his peasants, and he had duties of hospitality. Today, the rich man owes nothing, except the taxes he does not pay. Even in Eastern European countries, where only the "new classes" have the right to their "datchas," automobiles, and special stores, its reign is supreme. Certainly money is necessary in exchanges among men; its suppression is no more than a dream. Profit continues to indicate a business' health, but it gives us no information concerning the product's social usefulness or its importance for the common good. Profit must never become an abstract value; no more than the state, the party, or law and order can it be an absolute.

The cult of any of these pseudo-absolutes leads inevitably to the desire for revolution, a yearning found even in the Bible. The Magnificat, the canticle the evangelist Luke attributes to Mary once she learns she is pregnant with the Messiah, tells us that "God puts down the mighty from their thrones and raises up the humble . . . he fills the hungry with good things and sends the rich away empty." Following Jesus' famous denunciation of the rich, the apostle James cries out: "Woe to you rich, your wealth is rotten. The wages you have kept from the laborers cry out to heaven." If one really believes in the dignity of men/women, even violent revolutions are sometimes necessary. Prophetic indignation, recognizing as intolerable situations long regarded as normal, fans the fires of change. The most necessary of revolutions, however, needs to be disciplined by the art of politics lest it become an idol. No revolution settles everything, for evil is much wider and deeper than social, political, or economic conditions. When Maurice Clavel says it is very dangerous not to believe in original sin, he is not simply announcing a pious bromide. If we identify evil with one or another institution or situation, we tend to believe it will disappear once the situation is changed or the institution is overthrown. In reality, we let our defenses down and allow evil to rise up anew with another face. Brecht was right: the womb that produces monsters is still fecund. Idolized revolution leads to one of two conclusions: either it succeeds and tends to build up a system even more oppressive than the one it overthrew, or it fails and engenders despair. Only patient, realistic revolutionaries can build a better world.

To avoid becoming idols, revolutionary political systems need to ask themselves: "What is our idea of man?" Itself a Judaeo-Christian notion, revolution is totally unimaginable in an Islamic, Hindu, Buddhist, or Confucian context. For what reason would a Hindu, believing in the universal vanity of all things, revolt against the misery of his neighbor? Even the word revolution, which for the Greeks meant the eternal return of things, took on the significance of rupture, overthrow, and parousia only in the Judaeo-Christian tradition. It inspired the great poverty movements of the Middle Ages and, laicized by agnostic Jews still filled with the spirit of the Bible, gave life to the socialistic hopes of the 19th century. Marxists themselves do well to question why they refuse to turn their backs on the ancient tradition of the exploitation of the poor by the rich. In part, their idea comes from the biblical prophets, crying out for justice. But it comes, too, from the 18th century encyclopedists, with their abstract, simple, normative man. This ideal man then spawned a dangerously brutal child—the elimination or imprisonment of all who do not resemble him: the mentally ill, the weak, the lawbreakers. The only man/woman the revolutionaries and politicians must love is concrete man/woman: complex, contradictory, and suffering. Otherwise, revolution and politics disintegrate into another contraband religion.

The men of the Enlightenment, disdaining their passions and positing their normative man, also held that science and reason had taken religion's place. Certainly the gradual acquisition of rational, laicized knowledge marked great progress for humanity. It was good to de-sacralize man's thought, for religion never was intended to fill up the holes in rational inquiry and thereby limit intellectual pursuits. As Simone Weil wrote: "I cannot give the church any right to limit the operations of intelligence. If I did, I would commit a crime against my vocation which demands absolute intellectual probing." No church, party, or state has the right to limit the operations of rational scientific thought. Conversely, however, as Kant himself saw, there is something in religion that escapes the realm of science. Science looks to rational demonstration, but it has not begun to pretend that rational inquiry is the only possible meeting place between men/women and the world. The universe admits of other possibilities: the adoration of the mystic or the ecstasy of the poet or the artist. If science cannot prove beauty, does that mean that beauty does not exist? Science and reason can situate the poet in his/her era, milieu, or class struggle; they can take apart his/her words in structural fashion and even psychoanalyze him/her. But when all these operations are completed, what will have been said about beauty? The poet, the mystic, and the believer have something just as important to say as the rational scientist. In fact, the same individual can be scientific expert, poet, and mystic—I should have said: he/she must be. The truly scientific and rational person must have a healthy agnosticism so he/she can recognize other domains than science and reason and other possibilities than rational demonstration. Otherwise, science and reason become his/her idols, imprisoning his/her religious impulse. "Scientism" is not a bygone mentality; it is still the last word in Marxist thought. As a contraband religion, science and reason run the risks of castration and elitism. Castrating, they dry up a man so he becomes one-dimensional, reduced to his cerebral functions, like some science-fiction monster. Promoting elitism, they extend the myth that only the great researchers with access to the sources of scientific information are truly human; the weak and debilitated are not really men.

Nowhere perhaps are the ill effects of this elitism more apparent than in the domain of medicine. All the ingredients are present to produce one of the most beautiful contraband religions of the civilized world, with physicians as the last word in clergymen. The setup is this: often patients feel a deep need to forget a death that none of the contraband religions will allow them to face or overcome. Physicians in turn, falling prey to the god-like prestige science and reason know how to command, receive the homage and submission of their faithful. Recently I published the story of a mother whose child died of leukemia in a French hospital. The child was incurable. What was so shocking in her testimonial was the attitude of the physicians. They never spoke with her; they explained nothing; they never even saw her. If I call in a plumber or an architect, he/she comes with a knowledge I do not possess, but he/she does not feel obliged to hold me in contempt for my ignorance. He/she tells me how he/she plans to do what I have asked of him/her. Fortunately, many physicians, young and old alike, are trying to do away with this nefarious, elitist attitude that makes their profession little more than another contraband religion.

Religion and Ethics

Together with science and reason, ethics was the other pole of the Encyclopedists' religion. It must be said forcefully, however, that religion is not ethics. Here I separate myself absolutely from Henri Bergson who linked the two very closely. Ethics, like politics, is an affair of common sense, situation, and circumstance. For my part, I have never asked any clergyman to make my ethical decisions for me. Religion, of course, relates to ethics as the foundation of all practical action, be that scientific, political, or ethical. As foundation, however, it must not be confused with the action itself—nor must it prescribe practical formulas. Unfortunately, since stoicism has eaten away Christianity from the inside out, the Christian ethic is nothing more than duty and virtue. Marcus Aurelius has replaced Jesus Christ, and a living, vital Christianity filled with wisdom and folly, is no longer found except among a few madmen/madwomen and a few saints! Stoical Christianity, the ethic of effort and good resolutions, offers formula after formula to traumatize and embitter its people, since neither effort nor good resolution changes a man's/woman's heart. Religion and adoration do, since they enable man/woman to love and be loved. If a person's religion is no more than effort or good resolution, he/she will end up in anguish, rejecting all effort as sterile and a waste of time. St. Augustine summed up the Christian ethic as, "Love God and do what you will"—hardly an ethical formula!

It is tragic that Christianity was absorbed by stoicism, but just as tragic that Marxism, in its turn, has taken over the stoical idea of man/woman— corrected, of course, by large doses of Messianism. The Marxist states are as sad, boring, and castrating as any priest's boarding school. What will be left in China or Vietnam once the revolutionary messiahs have fallen? A religion of ethical order, or perhaps just the contraband religion of law and order and nothing more.

Sexuality and Art as Contraband Religions

Before finishing this list of contraband religions, I do not want to forget the two most common: sexuality and art. Since, as we have seen already in chapter three of this book, they are so closely akin to the religious impulse, they are much more difficult to distinguish from true religion than are the other contraband religions. For men and women today physical touch with another person is often the only contact with nature left in an entirely urbanized world and orgasm the only religious experience. The intellectuals, in their turn, look to art and aesthetics for a high quality substitute for religion. As we have already seen, however, neither sexuality nor art, no more than any other contraband religion, can deliver man from death.

An Abuse of Good Things

All of the realities just listed as contraband religions are good in themselves: the state is necessary, the party legitimate, order useful. Money allows for exchanges, politics gives room for the struggle, revolution makes for the overthrow of tyranies and the suppression of man's/woman's exploitation of man/woman. Ethics enables the common life. With reason and science man/woman develops his/her understandings. In the church he/she experiences communion with other people. In sex he/she plays and loves. In art he/she creates. Once made into a god, everyone of them becomes an imprisoning and human-devouring idol that only aggravates the religious impulse since none have the corrective of the transcendent. Identifying happiness with one or another institution is even more dangerous than putting happiness off until heaven, the poisonous attitude justly criticized by the Marxists. An idolized institution can no longer be reformed and ends up exterminating everything else. This great need to believe in a terrestrial paradise pushes many men and women to live these realities and institutions as religions. Playing with apocalypse and parousia, they dream of a perfect society with perfect order, building their castles around a life in common with no restraints or repressions. What is the difference between this "golden era" and the old earthly paradise of the catechism's Adam and Eve? Even the "wondrous evening" of Maoist China was one of God's days!

In reality, human beings are adult only when they admit, without falling into absolute pessimism, that earthly paradise does not exist and never will. With warm lucidity, they understand that nothing will ever be absolutely perfect, and they continue to fight on with what Abbe Pierre has called "enthusiastic disillusion."

Our consideration of the contraband religions and the ill effects of idolatry shows that the religious impulse of itself is ambiguous, capable of inspiring the best or the worst in humanity. One cannot dispose of it without risking devastating repression and neurosis. We come now to the key chapter of this book where we will answer the questions: Are there criteria for choosing from among the religions the one most truly liberating and fulfilling?

The Criteria of Choice in Matters of Religion

Since I am speaking in this book of the "good use" of religion, what do I mean by "good"? It should be clear by now that by "good" I mean whatever frees, encourages growth, and leads to fullness of life. By "bad" I mean whatever castrates, enslaves, and blocks communication— whatever flees from reality. Keeping these notions in mind, I have found seven criteria religion must have if it is to make "good use" of the religious instinct.

First, it must be conscious of its own identity. Christianity introduced a giant step in religious self-consciousness when it laicized the state, for centuries accepted non-critically as a religion. Like the other contraband religions listed in the previous chapter, the state failed to see how it misused man's/woman's capacity for adoration in encouraging him/her to adore just about anything. Nor could the state do what a religion must do: situate man/

49

woman in his/her universe and heal his/her anxiety. Religion is not society; when the state becomes a religion, confusion and idolatry reign supreme.

Second, a religion must not be idolatrous. Christianity sought to avoid this pitfall by introducing the distinction between the sacred and the profane, but this nuance ran its own risk, and, as the profane fell more and more under the domain of science, technology, and knowledge, the sacred found itself gradually reduced to the world of charms and pious amulets. In fact, such a distinction actually slays the religious impulse. The primitive Church of the patristic era knew no such distinction. It differentiated only between what was already sacred and what was yet to become sacred. If nothing on this earth was to be adored, it could all be sanctified, even the earth's most trivial or grossest realities. The Church fathers recognized a total autonomy for the world's institutions, but it saw within them all the mysterious and necessary presence of the holy.

Third, a religion must be non-sectarian. What arises here is the problem of truth and error. Must we renounce judgment on doctrinal content in the name of a certain vapid irenicism? Certainly not— especially as we seek criteria for a true religion. Non-sectarian religion will have two characteristics: (1) the recognition of large elements of truth in others different from itself, and (2) the refusal to condemn others supporting ideologies judged to be false. Sectarian religions, sharing in common their condemnatory attitudes for all who do not think as they do, proliferate in societies where there is little room for man's/woman's religious impulses, even in Iron Curtain countries. Enclosing their adherents in intellectual ghettos they fabricate fanatics; even certain political groupings are sectarian from this point of view. Truly non-sectarian religion looks first to the truth shared in common and then to the points of separation. As Thomas Aquinas (usually not suspect of excessively liberal ideas) wrote: "Whatever is true, no matter who says it, comes from the Holy Spirit." Emmanuel Mounier, in his turn, added: "In every error there is a parcel of truth that makes it live. We cannot war against that error unless we first recuperate that hidden parcel of truth."

Fourth, a religion must not be bigoted. Bigotry, a mixture of sugary sentimentality, infantile superstition, and low-grade magic, grows on religions as they get older. Its soft face has made Christianity disgusting to generations of adolescents, but its visage is also evident in Communist, military, and other laicized forms, one as revolting as the next. To avoid this illness, a religion must be strong, expressing itself with courage.

However important these criteria may be, they are only secondary in determining which religions ring true. The following three are fundamental.

Religions of Call and Religions of Authority

Marcel Légaut, following Bergson's classic distinction between static and dynamic religions, has pinpointed the most essential of the three when he writes of the difference between religions of call and religions of authority. Religions of authority, faithful to the teaching of Dostoevski's Grand Inquisitor, seek to transform men/women into submissive cattle. To assure that their power be maintained, they conduct their plan of action principally on the collective plane, usually trying to dominate the societies where they develop. Since they must remain immutable (for any change is a menace to authority), they are conservative and reactionary, preaching submission to all authority, whether clerical or not. With answers for everything, they look for nothing new. As guardians of every door, they neither seek, nor ask, nor knock. Religions of call, recognizing authority as a service limited by space and time, address themselves to the individual, seeking to awaken him/her, put him/her on the road, and place him/her face to face with his/her own responsibilities. Liberating religions, they often preach revolution against what is often established disorder. At the heart of all the great religious systems lies the dialectic between these two forms of religion. Christianity itself began as a spiritual, evangelical religion of call, but by the time of the Counter-Reformation it had become the papalized religion of authority. Even libertarian socialism, a religion of call in its early revolutionary and messianic days, degenerated shortly after 1917 into the heavy, reactionary religion of authority we call Stalinism. Of all the religions of call, the great prophetic movement constantly vibrating through

Judeao-Christian history against the forces of order and somnolence remains the richest.

Religion and the Present

In its second fundamental criterion, religion must be of the present. If it does not help the human person live intensely in the present world, religion will never give a zest or a taste for life. Nothing more empoisons a person than focusing her/his powers of adoration on a life and a world "beyond." As Marx pointed out, such promises, when offered the proletariat in return for their submission, engendered a hatred for life. When I became a Christian at the age of twenty and began to hear my Christian friends tell their horror stories about the education they received for the "other world," I understood better why my grandfather hated a religion so castrating. Christianity, of course, is not the only religion susceptible to this danger. Secular and political religions, with their mythical "golden era" of a better world, propose a "life beyond" just as debilitating as the ethereal paradise the good nuns set up in opposition to this "valley of tears." Entire generations have been sacrificed for the dreams of a "happy tomorrow," a tomorrow always pushed further and further away. One does not build future happiness on present misery . . . hopeless fathers beget bitter sons! Jesus, although his promise of a fulfilled life yet to come gave salt to the future, did not really prepare his disciples for a world beyond the present. He demanded that his disciples live their todays. "The kingdom of God is in your midst," he said. Even after the Ascension, the angel chided the apostles: "Why do you stand here looking up to heaven?" and encouraged them to return to the city where they lived.

Religion as Multi-Dimensional

Finally, to borrow Marcuse's barbarian phrase, a religion must be "multi-dimensional," taking into account man's/woman's horizontal, interior, and vertical aspects. The great pagan religions, stressing the horizontal dimension, found their absolutes in the exterior world of nature—animals, plants, fire, wind, the sea, springs, and sun and the moon—luminous forces isolated from the modern city dweller. Christianity, of course, de-sacralized the world of nature long ago, but modern man/woman, twisting this de-sacralization into lack of respect, began to rape and pollute this world. Strangely enough, when man/woman makes nature an absolute, he/she loses himself/herself in it; when he/she no longer respects nature, he/she destroys it. In either case, he/she remains alone, for in nature he/she never encounters his/her own image and likeness. A very primitive text in the book of Genesis speaks to this phenomenon: man, naming the animals, recognizes himself in none of them. Only with the appearance of another like himself—woman—does his heart thrill with joy. One-dimensional religion, over-stressing the horizontal aspect, encourages man to worship his own image. From this tendency arose the great humanistic brotherhoods of the 19th century, the epoch of the great "Internationals." Only the enormous force of the religious impulse can explain the messianic impact of Marxist socialism. Significantly, the same winds also waved the black flag of anarchy, with its exalted idea of the individual. Both socialism and anarchy represent the epitome of "horizontalized," one-dimensional religion, even though both are by-products of Christianity, the first real community in human history to emphasize the dignity of the individual person. Unfortunately, when religion focuses uniquely on what is exterior to humankind, it gives birth to cosmic beings with little personal consistency, dissolved in the very nature they adore. If religion over-stresses the brotherhood, its adherents become gregarious beings lost in the crowd. If it emphasizes the individual and nothing more, it produces beings locked into their own image, cut off from any personal heritage or history.

Religion and the Inner Life

Next comes the interior dimension. When the religious impulse follows the path within, it touches unfathomed depths in men and women. "God is closer to me than my very being!" exclaimed St. Augustine. Interior, spiritual men/women of all times witness to this invisible reality, more real for them than the exterior world of the horizontalists. The person who has not had the intense experience of this secret depth remains rootless, a person of flattened spirit. If a religion concentrates solely only this dimension, however, it produces magnificent schizophrenics, totally indifferent to the sufferings and struggles of their contemporaries. India, for instance (and the majority of the Oriental religions) continues to fascinate the young of the West by its emphasis on the inner life. But how do they bypass Hinduism's disdain for action and its disinterest in history? Its attitude bears enormous responsibility for the social rottenness into which the subcontinent continues to sink, One day an Indian Mao-Tse-Tung will rise up to replace the religion of his fathers with a Promethean religion from the West. India will then lose her soul, but she will no longer die of starvation.

Third, there is the vertical dimension. With the advent of monotheism religion began to lean progressively toward the transcendent and follow the vertical path. Monotheism, when its idea of God is neither the divine policeman nor the sadistic father, frees the human person, drawing him/her to higher things. No longer bound to adore the things of this world or her/his own image or even the spirit within, she/he become free with regard to them all. If religion finds itself locked up totally in the "beyond," however, it raises up believers too little sensitive to life on earth. Remaining strangers to the great universal movements, they stand horrified by the legitimate revolutions against oppression and misery. From this point of view, certain forms of Judaeo-Christianity and Islam stand for reproach;

God is Lord, they say, and he crushes just about everything.

The Great Religions Integrate Human Life

The great religions, therefore, will be judged according to their capacity for integrating all these dimensions of human life. Christianity, in its earliest days, promulgated belief in a God bringing together all three dimensions—a Father "above and beyond," a brother "around and about," and a Spirit "within." This famous doctrine of the Trinity is not much in vogue today; one imagines a shamrock or some sort of theological algebra. The true Christian, however, knows she/he can find in this statement of belief a God at once Father, Brother, and Spirit. Too often in contemporary Christianity, the conservatives' "vertical" religion stands in opposition to the progressives' "horizontal" religion, and truly "interior" Christians are hard to find at all!

To make "good use" of the religious impulse, a religion must be conscious and aware, imposing no obligations to adore any of this world's realities. Tolerant and strong, it must be multi-dimensional, a religion of the present and a religion of call. Certainly none of the great historical religions nor any of the modern contraband religions is perfectly good or totally bad. At the heart of them all struggles the dialectic between the powers of freedom and the forces of sclerosis. Each of us must choose the religion that suits us best, using the criteria we judge most appropriate for ourselves. One question still lingers: Has there ever been one religion that responded to these criteria for the good use of religion? Did there arise, however furtively, one perfectly freeing religion? If so, would it not be worthwhile to try to find it once again?

A Freeing Religion

The Person of Jesus

When I sought to quench my thirst for truth in the philosophers and the great religions, my grandfather's influence made it impossible for me to adhere to any one of them until the day I rose above the prejudices of my milieu and opened the Gospels. The historical existence of Jesus of Nazareth was never a problem for me. Like André Malraux, I had always felt the personality of Jesus sufficiently believable because of the quality of the words ascribed to him. With Jung, I had always understood that he must have possessed a personality endowed with extraordinary energy to have fulfilled so perfectly the general longings of his time. Certainly the Gospels are not history books; they are partially mythicied and theologized catechisms. But behind them all lies the incomparable visage of the Nazarene. There are things, after all, that cannot be invented. These writings ring in a new sound and a unique message: "Never has anyone spoken as this man spoke," proclaimed his contemporaries, and those who continue to believe in him repeat the same theme. Jesus' message, to put it bluntly, remains profoundly blasphemous. I know that in writing that statement I will provoke an explosion from the conservatives, but I am inventing nothing. The Scribes and Pharisees spying on the prophet of Galilee said the same thing: "This man blasphemes." He did not, of course, blaspheme God; he blasphemed the idols, the contraband religions of his day.

Jesus blasphemed the temple, turned into an idol by his contemporaries. To the Samaritan woman he said: "Believe me, woman, the hour is coming when neither on this mountain nor in Jerusalem will you worship the Father . . . the hour is coming, and now is, when the true worshipers will worship the Father in spirit and in truth."

The clergy and the Scribes also heard his blasphemy. "They tell you what to do," he charged, "but they do nothing themselves. They lay heavy burdens on men's shoulders, but refuse to lift a finger themselves." The priest and the levite saw the wounded man in Jesus's story and continued on their way; Jesus called the leaders of the people "whitened sepulchers."

Jesus blasphemed authority, refusing to admit they were to be revered or adored. To his disciples he said: "Call no one father—because you are all brothers, call no master." When the apostles disputed over the highest places, he gave them this lesson: "You know that those who are supposed to

rule over the Gentiles love to lord it over them . . .
but whoever would be great among you must be
your servant, and whoever would be first among
you must be the slave of all."

Although he maintained a great respect for the
Jewish Law, Jesus advocated great liberty with regard to its prescriptions: "Hypocrites," he said,
"which of you, if he has a sheep and it falls into a pit
on the Sabbath, will not lay hold of it and lift it
out?" Nor did he bend to the regulations governing
ritual purity: "for what renders a man impure is not
what he eats, but what comes out of his heart." He
constantly taught his disciples: "The letter kills, but
the Spirit gives life," a phrase St. Paul would take up
in his turn.

Against the idolatry of Jewish chauvinism,
Jesus declared he had not found faith in all of Israel
like that of the Roman centurion; he offered as
model the heretical Samaritan who helped the
wounded man the Jewish priest and levite passed
by. Nor did Jesus tolerate the idolatry of money,
saying it was "easier for a camel to pass through the
eye of a needle than for a rich man to enter the
kingdom of heaven." To his astounded disciples he
declared: "One cannot serve both God and money."

Jesus especially blasphemed the established
ethic. In his parables he told of the eleventh hour
worker who gained as much as the laborer who
worked the whole day long; he praised the prodigal
child more than his elder brother who had never
wasted his heritage on loose living. He even dared
to throw this censure to the proper folk of his day:

61

"The prostitutes will precede you into the kingdom of heaven." Why?—Because for Jesus the love of God is always a gift; it can never be merited by ethical behavior. Gratitude can be merited, perhaps, but not love. Don Quixote learned he could conquer all the windmills of Castile without winning any right over Dulcinea's heart.

When he overthrew the tables and chased the moneylenders from the temple, crying that they had changed the house of prayer into a den of thieves, the chief priests and Scribes sought to destroy him. To their hostility Jesus replied openly and candidly: "Woe to you, scribes and pharisees, hypocrites! for you the mint and dill and cumin, and you have neglected the weightier matters of the law—justice, mercy, and faith . . . these you ought to have done, without neglecting the others. You blind guides, straining out a gnat and swallowing a camel!— brood of vipers!" Was Jesus a Palestinian Che Guevara as Judas Iscariot, the zealot, believed? No, he did not give political advice. He left his disciples alone on the political decisions, sending them back to their own consciences. When a certain man asked him to settle a dispute between him and his brother, Jesus replied: "Who set me up as judge over you?" In my opinion, Judas did not betray Jesus for thirty pieces of silver; rather, he sought to force his master's hand in turning him over. Then, he hoped, Jesus would cross his Rubicon and take power. Of course, Jesus did nothing of the kind. He allowed himself to be arrested, tortured, and crucified, going to the end with his apparently absurd nonviolence.

Jesus cried forth consistently, in and out of season, his fundamental message that life, not death, is the last word about existence, that disdain and hatred can be overcome in forgiveness, and that God loves all men/women, calling them, virtuous or not, to share in the freedom of his scandalous love. If Jesus blasphemed, he did so in the great prophetic tradition, blaspheming the idols. The apostle John, "the disciple whom Jesus loved," when he had grown old, understood well his master's message as he repeated over and over again: "My little children, beware of idols!" Jesus is not a great political revolutionary, but he is history's greatest de-mythologizer and de-sacralizer, fighting untiredly that religion be given its rightful place. Neither law, nor the state, nor money, sex, nor any other earthly reality is worthy of adoration. All are good; none are god. None are to be made into idols.

Nothing brought home more clearly Jesus's teaching than his word about the Sabbath, the Mosaic Law's most sacred institution. Contesting neither its legitimacy nor its usefulness, he uttered the liberating phrase that has made the Gospels a subversive message for all time: "The Sabbath is made for man, not man for the Sabbath." For this word, "Sabbath," we can easily substitute any of the realities we have labeled the "contraband" religions: the state, the party, the Church, law and order, money, revolution, science, ethics, sexuality, and art. They are made for people, not people for them. Anyone who hears the message of Jesus is free with regard to them all. The Roman empire, well aware of the Gospel's subversive character, persecuted the early Christians because of Jesus' universal de-sacralization, including his stand against the cult of the state. The empire tolerated all religions and received all gods into its pantheon, but it called the Christians atheists, since Christians denounced the gods as idols. In a sense, the charge is true—there is a refusal of idolatry in every atheism, and Christians will continue to be denounced as atheists by totalitarian powers, on the condition, of course, that they remain Christian.

Jesus' Spirit and Modern Christianity

Unfortunately, very little of Jesus' spirit remains in modern Christianity. Jesus's subversive message, smothered by the weight of ecclesiastical apparatus, finds itself transformed into a religion of authority, and its very existence is in danger. As Marcel Légaut affirmed: "Christianity finds itself cornered, driven to a mutation built into its origins against which its history, however, constantly rebels." We need to reflect on this law of historical entropy which says that everything degenerates, breaks down and ultimately betrays itself. To avoid falling into bitter skepticism, believers find hope in their conviction that re-birth, renewal, and the arising of new fidelities depend on them.

In reading the Gospels for the first time at the age of eighteen, I understood I had at last found the way. At forty, I know from experience this way is still good. Only in the Gospels can the good use of religion be found. Jesus, however, was not speaking just for himself. He spoke for a transcendence, making us understand that when we give God his rightful place, approaching him as he is to be approached, he neither crushes us down nor exalts us to the skies—he frees.

What Transcendence?

When the anarchists of the last century cried "Neither God nor Master!" they were rightly denouncing the pagan god most Christians then revered. The Judaeo-Christian god, originally a bedouin tribal deity scarcely distinguishable from other pagan divinities, developed gradually into the God of Jesus Christ, largely through the immense prophetic and Gospel adventure. In the nineteenth century and still today, God has once again become a pagan idol—the "policeman" god to guarantee social and moral order, the "magician" god nourished on fear, the "plug-all-the-holes" god to explain what science and reason do not, the "all-powerful" god responsible for everything in the world, including evil. This god's primary purpose is the engendering of servility and submission; he is the sadistic father born of early childhood frustrations, a re-incarnation of Voltaire's Great Clockmaker. The old anarchists were wrong in confusing God with his caricatures; their cry should have been: "Neither idol nor Master!" a challenge

66

Jesus never ceased throwing to the servile, idolatry-prone crowds that thronged about him. In the naivete of the 19th century, of course, there was no way of realizing that religion was not dying, but simply rising again to wear new and more dangerous masks. The thinkers of that century did not understand that the only way to avoid excesses in religion is to give the religious impulse its proper place.

The Effects of Religion

Religion will always produce one of two effects: it either releases a transcendence or reinforces a given social or moral order. The first effect, taking away all the fatalities that weigh upon a man, subverts suffocating law and frees the human person. The second, defending established order, heals human anxiety only at the price of personal liberty. A religion of call produces the first effect; a religion of authority strives for the second. The most subtle religions of authority try to make transcendence the very basis of the institutions they defend, a difficult operation to be sure, since even the blindest of men can see the faults in the most venerable institutions. When defense of the institution itself becomes impossible, religions of authority then speak of the transcendent in terms of the "life and world beyond." God becomes the absolute with a perfection that exists nowhere but serves well as the basis and foundation for all existing order— precisely the religious illusion denounced by Marx and Feuerbach! How dangerous this illusion can be!

The idea of the absolute must never descend into the sphere of power, no matter what that power may be. True transcendence is not a Platonic idea of perfection; it is the basis for none of this world's social or moral orders.

The God of Jesus Christ

The transcendent God announced by Jesus Christ is not a projection, as Feuerbach claimed, nor even Jung's "archetype," pre-existing our collective unconscious. The God of Christianity can be identified with nothing in the universe, for nothing is more sacred than he. The person believing in this God finds himself beyond slavery; his thirst is for the absolute, and he finds no absolute in this world. He carves a cave of dissatisfaction in the human person that sparks liberty. With the Beatitude the believer says: "Blessed are those who hunger and thirst for the righteousness of God." Paul the apostle, in his turn, sings of the "glorious freedom of the children of God." Nor is this transcendent God dwelling simply in a world or a life "beyond." He is, in fact, at the heart of all reality, but identified with none. Jesus, with all the religious mystics of all time teaches that no institution, no matter how prestigious, nor any experience, however strong, can pretend to capture God. Yes, they express God, but fleetingly—if we try to adore them, God will leave, and we will be left with little more than a cadaver to worship.

Because this transcendent God is so elusive, all

theology about him since Jesus must be negative. Nothing we can say about God defines him, not even the philosophical notions of perfection. We can say simply that he is not what we think him to be. The Fathers of the Church understood this idea well, as John Damascene wrote: "God is infinite and incomprehensible, and the only thing we can say about him is his infinity and his incomprehensibility. Everything we do say about him is inadequate. God is not like other beings—not that he does not exist, but that he is above all beings, even above being itself." Damascene tells us that God resides where our concepts have no access. If we wish to speak about him we can do so only poetically.

Negative theologizing, however, does not lead to Buddhism's empty absence. If rational speculation is powerless to reach God, mystical contemplation is not. Believers have this experience. God awakens them, and they wrestle with him as Jacob wrestled with the angel. Because of God, believers begin their pilgrimage toward an unknown land, as did Abraham. They risk their lives and never allow themselves to be stopped by failure. "Men of desires" reach him—men of whom the Book of Revelation spoke long before Lacan. Desire, so popular with modern psychoanalysts, is what God hollows out in the human heart.

Dennis the Areopagite wrote: "Even he who desires the worst of lives, insofar as he desires to live the life that seems best to him, has, by that very desire, a part with God. It is a desire to live and a tendency toward life." In desiring, the human person keeps on growing and moves out beyond herself/himself. Going beyond his/her present, her/his desire increases, becoming more and more unquenchable. Man/woman must not repress desire, and, if it is true, as Dennis the Areopagite wrote, that all desire is ultimately for God, man's/woman's only wisdom is never to be satisfied with anything less. The believer will find that corresponding to his/her desire is an unspeakable fullness that heals him/her of anxiety and death. The nonbeliever will find her/his desire hollowed out in the obscure cloud of agnosticism. Like the believer, he/she will be free, for his/her religion, too, springing forth like a fountain, will never more imprison him/her in the bonds of idolatry.

We can never do away with adoration, and I keep telling myself every day how much better it is to adore the God of Jesus Christ than money or Mao.